Discovering Your Authentic Core Values

A step-by-step guide

Discovering Your Authentic Core Values

A step-by-step guide

Marc Alan Schelske

PO Box 220213   Portland   Oregon   97269

Published in Portland, Oregon by Live210 Media.

Edited by Tim Lale, Lale Editorial Services LLC

ISBN 978-0-9886882-0-9

Table of Contents

Special Thanks

I've written for a long time, but there is something different about crossing over from someone who writes to being a writer. It's a harrowing passage that wouldn't be possible without a lot of support and encouragement.

Christina Schelske: The making of a marriage from two independent-minded hearts is a big job. Thank you for sticking with me in this difficult but beautiful work. Your encouraging words mean the world to me, especially when you share your belief in me.

Bridge City Community Church: You are a stalwart community of faith that I so deeply love. Thank you for encouraging me to use my gifts and giving me the space to write.

Twitter, Facebook, and blog commenters: In this new era of digital communication, every book comes with a group of followers, fans, encouragers, challengers and friends. Without people engaging me on Twitter, Facebook and on my blog, I would not have the platform to share these thoughts. Without your engagement, questions and push-back what I write would not be nearly as good. Thank you for following, for reading, for sharing, for commenting and for continuing to show up. You are a blessing to me. I hope that I can be one to you.

Cindy Brosh: Thanks for being such a wise, compassionate and often painfully truthful counselor. You are proving to be instrumental in my growth, and certainly the things I'm learning in my process with you underlie every sentence of this book.

Kim Puckett: Thanks for editing and for using this process yourself. I'm so thankful to know such a creative and intentional woman.

Candi Burton: Thanks for editing in purple glitter pen. You know how much I like glitter. Thanks even more for the great feedback about how this process goes over in a family, and how I could make the process more gentle and coaching.

Connie Smith: Thanks for volunteering and for your deeply encouraging words.

Clint & Kate Hartwig: Thanks for your sharp eye, your many reminders about my tendency to start sentences with the word "but," and your counsel on how I can make the process feel less overwhelming.

This book was edited by **Tim Lale,** whom I recommend for his great attitude, incredible speed, and competence. Contact Tim if you need editorial services. Thank you, Tim, so much for making me look good!

Tim Lale Editorial Services, LLC / 208-890-3538 / tjlale@gmail.com

one

Why Core Values?

*It's not hard to make decisions
when you know what your values are.*

—Roy Disney

You want your life to be different than it is. That's why you're reading this book. Maybe one of these describes your situation:

- You're contemplating a new career that lines up more with your values and dreams.

- You've made a mess of your relationships and want things to be different.

- You're feeling stagnant and wish your life could have more energy.

- Your time is over-booked, your emotional bank account is overdrawn, and you need to focus.

- You want to make a difference in the world, doing good (or serving God, or however you would describe it), but you just don't know where to start.

Regardless of why you want to make a change, the question that matters is this: What change will you make?

For years, a standard tool for focusing organizations has been a list of *core values*.* These values, just a handful of simple statements, serve as a kind of rudder keeping the organization on track. When decisions have to be made, organizations can turn to their *core values* and know when to say yes and when to say no.

Service organizations and churches accomplish their missions more effectively when they are intentional. Companies are more profitable when they keep a tight focus. This makes great sense.

Why would we choose intentional practices for our companies and churches but not for our own lives?

Tools for intentional living

We understand this concept in the more practical areas of our lives. For example, both budgets and calendars are tools for intentional living. They provide personal accountability so we don't double-book our time or overspend our money.

As important as that is, they both do something even more vital. A budget and a calendar allow us to set the agenda for our money and time. They prevent us from being reactive. They also protect our resources from being directed by someone else's agenda.

You are surrounded by companies, marketing agencies, and other people who all have an agenda for your money. In the same way, you are surrounded by people and needs that want to monopolize your time. Deciding ahead of time on a budget, or a calendar plan, lets you set the agenda for your limited resources.

Our values are much less concrete than our time and money, but the arena of values and priorities works the same way. The world is full of competing values and principles. The people around you are all

---

* When you come across an italicized word like this, you'll find it in a glossary of terms at the back, with a more in-depth definition.

living out of certain values—whether they know it explicitly or not. If you don't get clear about your personal values, you will always be living in reaction to the value-based choices of the people around you. Either their values will shape your life, or your reactivity to their choices will. Neither of those is a life-giving, motivating, or dream-building way to live. God didn't design you to live in constant reaction to others.

If you want to make a change in your life, moving you into a more life-giving future, then having clear *core values* is an essential tool.

A compass, a water filter, a homing pigeon

More than ever before, we are faced with large and small decisions that affect our lives and the lives of the people around us. Decisions come at us faster and faster. In any given moment, we feel the stress of being pulled in many competing directions.

Once you've done the work of articulating your *core values*, you will have an invaluable aid for an intentional life. How? Think of three things: a compass, a water filter, and a homing pigeon.

A compass.

When you're navigating through decisions, competing commitments will often make it hard to choose which path to take.

Once, I chose to help someone I knew who was in need. My help included some financial support. Part of that money I considered to be a gift; another part I expected to be repaid. We had verbal discussions about this, and I thought we were on the same page. As time passed, it became clear that this person didn't plan on repaying me. Several awkward conversations revealed that we had different expectations.

At this point I was in a bind between two urges. On the one hand, it felt like the right thing to do was to confront the person and ask for repayment. I had gone well beyond my initial commitment in helping them. They needed to take responsibility. On the other hand, I had misstepped by not having a written agreement with them. I thought we were both on the same page, but we weren't. So I had made a mistake too. I could, on that basis, let the debt go. Both approaches seemed right. I had emotional energy pushing in both directions.

One of my personal core values is redemption. I define it this way:

Redemption

Forgiveness creates the space for people, relationships and opportunities to be restored, opening the door to a better future.

I was caught between two competing influences. This this core value pointed the way for me. I wanted to redeem this complicated situation. How could I open the door to a better future?

I decided to share with the person exactly what had happened for me. I was honest about how I had invested much more money than I intended, and now I felt taken advantage of. I shared that I realized we saw the situation differently and that I had failed to write down our agreement. This allowed me to state my truth and feel heard. It also created the space for the other person to feel heard. Then I forgave the debt because I wanted to create a second chance for the relationship.

My wife and I decided that all such agreements with others in the future would have to be written down. This would create a better future for me, for my family, and for anyone that we entered into agreements with.

Because all of this was in alignment with my core value, I was able to move forward without anxiety or second-guessing. This path felt right in my gut, in spite of the competing influences. It was in alignment with who I am and who I want to be.

Having personal core values is like having a compass in your pocket. When things get confusing, you can pull it out and re-orient yourself.

A water filter.

All of us are faced with countless decisions every day. We have more opportunities presented to us than we can possibly take. Sometimes our struggle is not to choose a good thing over a bad one; it's choosing which good thing to do with our limited resources.

Because there are so many opportunities for the investment of our time, money, and emotional energy we can easily over-extend ourselves. In fact, I wonder if an enormous portion of the dissatisfaction that people feel in their lives comes from this very problem. Most of us live over-extended lives, and we're not even sure how we got there. Core values act as a filter, not just for finding the right outcome, but more importantly for making sure we are asking the right questions.

Once the kids are asleep and the house quiets, I like to unwind. I've used that last hour of the day in a lot of different ways. My wife and I have watched movies or TV shows. I've spent time scrolling through Facebook or surfing interesting blogs. I'm also a big reader; I have been all my life. However, with a 6-year-old and a 4-year-old, I don't have the luxury of a lot of extra time.

One of my core values is growth. I express it like this:

Growth
Growing spiritually, emotionally, interpersonally, intellectually and in competence is the sign of a deeply engaged and healthy life.

When I think about how to spend the last hour of my day, this value challenges me. Instead of having to decide between countless options, this value filters the options for me.

I want to end the day doing something that helps me grow. It could be a conversation with my wife that grows our relationship. It could be reading a book or blog that tackles an area of my life where I want to grow or presents something I want to learn. Staying connected to the core value of growth screens out a pile of other options, keeping me focused on the things I care about most.

A homing pigeon.

Homing pigeons, also called messenger pigeons, have the uncanny ability to find their way back to their roost. They can fly vast distances, crossing difficult and unfamiliar geography, yet they nearly always find their way home. Something inside of them guides them back.

If you've done the hard work of articulating your true inside-out values, they will function the same way. Authentic core values draw you inexorably back to who you are supposed to be.

For the past few years I've been struggling with focus, motivation, and even depression. I was trying everything I could to make a change. Nothing seemed to be working.

In the course of counseling, I was reminded of how important creativity has always been in my life. It was central to me when I was a child. It's been vital at every point in my life where I've felt energized, effective, and purposeful, but in my depression I had stopped doing almost anything creative.

In my core value process, I identified that I have a core value of creative intentionality. I think of it like this:

Friends and my therapist counseled me to begin doing creative things again. So I did. I started playing my guitar. I began doing more visual art. I began to take my writing seriously and re-invigorated my blog. As I did that, I began to feel a renewed focus and passion. This core value led me back to something I had lost, something that had previously been a core part of who I am. Any healthy and effective future for me will include this value, and I had been wandering away from it.

Your values, your life

These examples show some of the ways that core values can help move you forward, but my core values won't help you. No matter how much you like my words, they aren't your own. Searching for "core values" online and copying the statements you like best won't work. Writing up a list of qualities you admire won't help you either. Why?

There are two kinds of core values. One of them is much more effective than the other.

two

Two Kinds of Core Values?

Your beliefs become your thoughts. Your thoughts become your words. Your words become your actions. Your actions become your habits. Your habits become your values. Your values become your destiny.

—*Mahatma Gandhi*

When core values go wrong

A list of core values is a helpful tool for an intentional and wholehearted life. Unfortunately having a well-articulated list of qualities that you hope to live by doesn't get the job done. If you already have a list of core values, you must ask yourself this question:

What it is that you really have on that list?

Many years ago, a large church was seeking a new senior pastor. During the search process the church leaders made it clear that the church had a core value of outreach. They wanted to grow and reach new people. This value figured prominently in their conversations with potential candidates. They finally hired a leader who shared that core value. He was passionate about the mission of reaching new people.

But then something unexpected happened. That new pastor began making changes so that the church could more effectively reach people. (What?!) It started with a few changes to the worship service. Then came a few changes to church governance. Old processes were questioned and changed. The changes worked. New people started showing up! But there was a problem. These new people were different.

That's when the truth emerged.

Resistance, undermining behavior, and exclusivism in some corners of the church bubbled to the surface. An influential group within the church didn't really want to grow, at least not like this. They wanted their old processes and expectations back. It seemed from their words that they actually wanted to be safe, surrounded by people just like them.

Their actions were radically different from what they had expressed in the pastoral search. They said that they held a core value of outreach, but that word on a piece of paper, no matter how strong the ideal had been in their minds, was entirely disconnected from what it seemed they really wanted.

Two kinds of core values?

What most people don't understand is that there are really two different kinds of core values:

▸ *Authentic Core Values*

▸ *Aspirational Core values*

The vast majority of core value lists floating around are *aspirational core values*. They are values that the person or company ardently wants to be true. They are qualities that the person admires and aspires to, but they are not currently true statements of reality. They may be an ideal. They may be a hope. But they are not the truth.

In the best case, an aspirational core value isn't a bad thing; it's a great tool for casting vision. It's a positive statement reflecting something we want to become one day. Values like this can also be called *Outside-In Core Values*. They are imposed from the outside or from above, with the hope that the internal reality will come into alignment with the value over time. Without very hard work and accountability, though, this just doesn't happen.

Unless you are clear in your mind that your values are aspirational, such values can be a problem. Having created a core value statement, you might think you've done the hard work. In reality, you've just created a list of hopes. That list of hopes can, without care, mask the real values that are driving you or your organization.

Who you really are is who you really are

Authentic core values are (unfortunately) the more powerful kind. Why? Because you already live according to your core values. Every day. Show me your life, and I will show you your core values. Core values are core because they reside at the center of who you are, shaping your thoughts and actions. Even if you never draw up a list of core values and print it on fancy paper, they are what is already functioning within you. These can also be called *inside-out core values*.

These are the qualities and desires that really, truly motivate your current behavior. Sometimes these values lead to wonderful, noble acts. Other times they lead to choices that you're ashamed of. They represent what is authentically true about you, both light and shadow.

Here's an example: I have an authentic core value of Redemption. Sounds good, right? Especially for a pastor. I've experienced powerful reconciliation in my life and seen how transformative it can be. I've thought long and hard about the ethics, philosophy, and theology of forgiveness. I even have the example and teaching of Jesus to validate and guide this value.

Years ago, I had the brutally painful experience of being profoundly betrayed by two close friends. My heart was crushed. There were serious consequences in my life and circle of relationships. Yet, as I wept and worked through the pain and grief, this value was one of the things that kept me from falling off the rails.

When the grief had finally run its course, I was able to experience reconciliation with these two friends. While our relationship is much different now, that experience was transformative for me. That's an example of this value of Redemption leading me well.

Another time, I found myself caught up in a controversy around behavior that I and some others found offensive and hurtful. I knew I needed to have some conversations with the people involved. I felt the sense of urgency in my heart that I've come to recognize as an important intuition, maybe even God's prompting. At the same time, I didn't want to see these friends alienated from each other.

At the time it seemed like avoiding the conflict would allow us to move more quickly toward reconciliation. What happened instead was that the damage grew worse. Even more people ended up being hurt. I allowed this value of Redemption (or a self-justifying version of the value) to lead me to a choice I am still sad about.

Here's what's true about your *authentic core values*: They motivate the choices you make—both good and bad choices. These are not a set of hopeful ideals that some imagined better version of yourself lives by. These are the real values at the core of who you are.

So why not aspire?

I want to suggest that your *authentic core values* are more important than any values you aspire to. How can this be? Doesn't this undermine the idea of life change?

I don't think so. Here's why. If you want to change, you have to know where you're starting. Wanting to travel to Chicago isn't enough. You have to know where you're starting from so you can plan the trip.

This is the same for core values. For example, I may aspire to be a forgiving person, but until I understand that I am liable to use forgiveness as a mask for avoiding conflict, I can't grow more healthy in my relationships. Instead of becoming a more forgiving person, I'll become someone who "gives in" to avoid conflict or who quickly "forgives" in order to be superior, or to be liked, or for some other self-justifying reason.

Once I know that this is true of me, I have the ability to evaluate the situation I am in. I can decide whether I am avoiding necessary conflict or seeking true reconciliation. Knowing this has allowed me to become much more authentically forgiving; I can forgive without held-back bitterness or resentment.

Why does this matter?

Identifying your *authentic core values* is incredibly important if you want to live an intentional life.

▸ Knowing what drives you allows you to be thoughtful about your actions, instead of living through your reactions.

▸ Knowing that your values have a shadow side allows you to be aware and step away from harmful choices, knowing what you could do and choosing not to do it.

▸ Naming your values allows you to re-envision a better, healthier future for yourself. This won't be an idealized imagined future, but a real future connected to who you actually are, where your God-given best self gets more of the stage time.

In eighteen years of working with people in spiritual growth and transformation I've seen this: When people grow, sometimes they become something altogether different than what they were before. But not always.

More often than not, they become a better, more focused, more life-giving version of who they were to begin with. If you believe that God wires us up from the beginning, as I do, that would only make sense. The Bible talks a lot about redemption, not much about transmutation.

Ephesians 2:10 says this: "For we are his workmanship, created in Christ Jesus for good works, which God prepared beforehand, that we should walk in them" (ESV). I believe this means that you were created by God's own hand as a work of divine art. You were made for a good and beautiful purpose. This is already embedded within you and your story, where God is waiting to bring it to light.

If you're wanting a more intentional life or a deeper, more life-giving spiritual journey, then getting clear about the values that drive you is an important place to start. If you're ready for the focusing clarity that comes with knowing your values, I'd like to walk you through the steps that will help you identify and articulate your authentic inside-out core values.

three

Gather Your Tools

There are no shortcuts to any
place worth going.

—*Beverly Sills*

Gather your equipment

You are who you are. If there's a better you out there to become, you'll find it by traveling from where you are now to where you could be. That means knowing who you are now. This is the purpose of identifying your *authentic core values*. If you're ready, then let the journey begin.

As with any great adventure, before we head out, you'll need to get some gear ready.

Bring your brain.

This is a reflection process. You will be thinking. That means you need your brain engaged. Sounds easy, since you always have it with you. However, if it's occupied with other complicated things, it will be hard for you to get good results. If you're in a lot of pain, if you're under enormous stress, or if the house is full of loud music or rambunctious toddlers, you're going to have a difficult time.

So, set your urgent stresses on the shelf for the moment and find a quiet place where you can focus. If your daily life is too complicated for that, then you probably need to schedule an overnight retreat of some kind. It doesn't have to be at an expensive location. It just needs to be away, where you will not be tempted to attend to the day-to-day.

Bring some kind of journal.

Part of reflecting is capturing your thoughts so you can work with them. In this step-by-step process you're going to have a number of assignments. That's going to take writing things down. So, get yourself a *journal*.

I use two different kinds. For old-school writing, I use the classic lined *Moleskine journal*. These are available online and at your local bookstore. I also use an online tool called *Evernote*. It's easy to use. I can access it from any computer as well as my other devices. The notes are infinitely searchable and tag-able and thus easy to find. The basic account, which will serve most people's needs, is free.

But those are *my* choices. You need to use what works for you. I have a friend who swears by yellow legal pads and blue Papermate pens. He's wrong, of course, but it works for him.

Whatever kind of journal you like, bring it with you. You're going to need it.

Give it time.

This process isn't quick. If you want good results you're going to have to think, reflect, write and digest. You need to be able to do it without many distractions. You're going to need to set aside a few blocks of time. Don't worry if this process takes you a while. The more you think about this, the better your results will be.

Be Honest.

OK, time for a quick heart-to-heart.

There's always a temptation when doing something self-reflective to see an edited-for-the-public view of ourselves. When we take personality inventories, for example, we sometimes answer the questions according to what we'd like the answer to be, rather than what is actually true. This risk is stalking you right now.

It's easy to start thinking about aspirational values rather than what is really true of us. Don't go down that path. Our goal is to bring to the surface the core values that are authentic to you, that come from your inside out. In order to get a useful result that will both resonate with your heart and take you to a better future, you've got to be deeply, brutally honest about yourself.

If you aren't ready to do that, you really aren't ready to grow. So, take a deep breath and decide. If you're ready to be honest, then you're ready to start.

four

Find the Clues in Your Story

*Life is a succession of lessons which must be lived
to be understood.*

—Ralph Waldo Emerson

Your inside-out values aren't very far away from you right now. They are a deeply embedded part of you.

Our first task is to surface the possibilities. Your *authentic core values* have been a part of your life since you were young. In many cases, they grew from seeds planted in childhood experiences. They've been shaping your life and guiding your decisions—both the good ones and the not so good ones.

Your story is where we turn. Your story is the narrative you hold about your life. It includes all your memories of the events that have happened to you and the meaning you took from those events, good or bad.

Your *authentic core values* are hidden here, within the details of your story.

Assignment 1

Find the clues in your story

1. Clear a space and a time for remembering.

Your first step is taking an inventory of the important choices and turning points in your life. This can be a lengthy process. I took several hours over the course of a couple of days to do this step and the next. So, block out some time and space to get alone with your journal.

2. List the emotionally important moments in your life.

Start today, and work backward as far back as you remember. Jot down any *emotionally important moment* that you can recall.

An *emotionally important moment* for our purposes is any important choice or turning point in your life you can remember clearly. If you can remember it clearly, there is something significant about it. Why? The intensity of our memories is linked to the emotional content of the memory. Everything you remember clearly has some kind of emotional context to it. These ought to be experiences in which you made a choice or reacted to something.

Your list should include:

▸ Big decisions you've made.

▸ Traumatic experiences in your life and your response to them.

▸ Critical points of transition in major relationships that you had a hand in.

▸ Any incident that you remember clearly where you made a choice that mattered.

This list ought to be fairly long. If you're thirty-five years old and you can only think of a single incident per year for the past twenty-five years, that means your list would be twenty-five items long. Chances are high you will have more than one important incident a year. If you end up with fifty to seventy-five memories you're getting in the ballpark.

For me this list included things like:

▸ Having my wife break up with me when we were dating, and how I responded.

▸ Choosing to adopt a son.

▸ Choosing to live in a community household.

▸ Reacting badly when my leadership was questioned in my job.

▸ Participating in a number of entrepreneurial nonprofit start-ups.

▸ A long-term relationship I've worked at with a very high-maintenance friend, even when other people suggested I ought to step back.

▸ A number of times I let myself be taken advantage of financially by people I cared about.

Don't worry too much about the details of each incident at this point. Your task right now is to just create a list of *emotionally important moments* where you made a choice. You don't need to write more than a sentence about each incident—just enough so that in the next assignment, you will know what memory you're referring to.

The assignment ends when you have a list that you feel represents as many of the critical decision-points and emotionally important experiences in your life that you can recall.

five

Consider the Why

Behind every trial and sorrow that He makes us shoulder, God has a reason.

— *Khaled Hosseini*

Remember, your core values are not values you hope one day will be true of you. These are the values and deeply held motivations that are already at work in your life.

You now have a few pages in your journal listing the *emotionally important moments* in your life when you made a choice or had a reaction. These are the significant incidents that shape your personal story. They are also the treasure chest in which you'll find your *authentic core values*.

Now we start to look beneath the surface. Why did these moments matter? More importantly, what motivation was showing up in these moments of your life?

Assignment 2

Consider the why

1. Clear a space for reflecting.

This may seem redundant, but it's critical that you don't rush this process. Take the time you need to think these things through. Your end result will be so much better, so much more true to who you are, if you give it the time necessary.

Remember that this kind of thinking is work. It has an emotional cost. Don't try to power through the whole thing in one sitting. If you find yourself getting tired or distracted, you've done enough. Put the project aside until the next block of time you've scheduled.

2. Take your moments one by one and ask, "Why?"

Proceed through your list of *emotionally important moments* and consider why each of those moments matters to you.

The fact that you remember these moments is not negligible. Our brains work through an associative process. Memories of every kind are made when different sensory input comes together in the brain, but the strong memories are strong precisely because there was an emotional component. The stronger the emotional element, the stronger the memory. So, while you may not be in touch with the emotional element of a particular memory today, the fact that you can clearly remember it means it was there at the time.

For each event, reflect and journal on why you reacted the way you did or made the choice you made. Consider questions like these:

- ▸ What internal problem was I trying to solve?
- ▸ What was I trying to avoid?
- ▸ What was I trying to accomplish?
- ▸ What was the emotional pay-off for me?
- ▸ Why did I choose this path, and not another?

3. Capture your motivation in a single word or phrase.

As you reflect on your motivation in each situation, try to narrow your reaction or choice down to a sound bite. You're looking for a single word or a short phrase of two or three words. Limiting yourself to just a couple of words means that you will not cover every nuance of the situation. It also requires that you push down to the essence of your motivation.

For example, one of my life events was choosing to adopt my son. I wrote in my journal about why this was important to me and brought a number of ideas to the surface.

- ▸ I'm adopted myself and wanted to pass on the belonging that was given to me.

- ▸ I know how adoption transformed my life and am aware that I have the power to effect that kind of change for someone else.

- ▸ Also, as an adopted child I have no blood relation to my family. Having an adopted child of my own was like finding "my tribe."

As I reflected on these different aspects of my decision, it seemed that all of these ideas centered around experiencing and creating belonging and new chances for myself or someone else. So, the key words I chose for this experience were "belonging," and "second chances."

Your goal is to tag each *emotionally important moment* in your original list with a single word or phrase identifying your motivation. Don't worry about choosing the right word or the most beautiful word. Don't worry if some of the words are negative or embarrassing. You're not thinking about core values yet. You're just thinking about motivations that have shown up in your life.

This assignment continues until you've been able to tag every one of your *emotionally important moments* in a way that seems fair or accurate to you. Once you've done that, congratulate yourself. You've already done a lot of good work.

Now we head somewhere you can only go with help.

six

Get the Unvarnished Outside View

Listen to counsel and receive instruction so that you may be wise.

—*Proverbs 19:20*

Here's a warning: this is the hardest assignment. After this, everything gets easier.

At this point, you have several pages in your journal identifying your *emotionally important moments*, each tagged with a key word or short phrase about your motivation in that situation. That's rich content. Shortly we will start mining it for your *inside-out core values*. First, however, we need a bit more material to work with.

One of the problems with being you is that you see through your own eyes. No matter how mature you are, or how elevated your perspective, you have blind spots that come as a result of being a human being trapped inside your own head. In order to really understand the values that have guided your life, you need some unbiased input.

This has to come from outside your head. Since your dog can't speak, that means going to other people.

This is the hardest part of the process. It requires a great deal of vulnerability, but if you will take it seriously and engage it non-defensively, it's also the part that will give you the best information for your process.

Assignment 3
Get the unvarnished outside view

1. Select your mirrors.

Brainstorm a list of people. These should be people who know you now, know you well, and ideally have known you over a long period of time. You want people who will be kind; this is not an invitation for others to bash you with their personal agenda. Even so, you want people who are willing to tell you the truth. The more carefully you select these people, the better feedback you will get.

For me it included people who work for me, people I have served for many years as pastor, close friends who have known me for more than twenty years, my therapist, and my wife.

You want a good-sized list if you can come up with it. Some portion of these people won't want or be able to participate, so you need to have enough people on your list that you'll still get good feedback. Somewhere between ten and fifteen is ideal. Don't settle for less than eight.

2. Invite your mirror's feedback.

Ask each of the people on your list to reflect on their experience of you and give you some feedback. You're asking them to share their experience of you, and to capture it in the top few motivations or values they see driving you and your decisions.

Give them clear instructions written in your own words. This needs to come from you and be appropriate for your relationship. Here's an example:

Hey Bill,

I'm sending this note to a number of my close friends and family members because I really value our relationship and your insight.

I'm going through a little book called **Discovering Your Authentic Core Values** as a project for my personal and spiritual growth, and I'd like your help. You see me from outside my head, which means you see me in ways that I don't get to see myself. If you're willing to give me some honest feedback on how you experience me, that would be a tremendous gift.

I'd like for you to email me a list of the things you think motivate me most, maybe 3-5 items. These can be positive or negative. They just need to be things that you believe motivate my choices and reactions. And please, tell me the truth.

For example, do you think I'm motivated by family or security or financial gain? What factors have you seen guide me in my relationships or other important choices?

For each one, it would be helpful if you'd give me a key word or phrase for the motivation (like family or loyalty or "being right") and then write a few sentences explaining an example or two where you've seen this in me.

I promise to simply listen to your feedback without defensiveness. I may contact you with some clarifying questions, but I won't question your experience or get defensive. I truly want to know the unvarnished truth about how you experience me. If you're willing to support me in this way, it would be really helpful to get your thoughts back by (such-and-such a deadline).

And if this feels uncomfortable or you don't have time to do it or really any reason at all, please don't feel burdened by my request. If you have any questions, please call or email. I'd love to talk about it.

Thank you.

Take courage and then press the "Send" button.

3. Prepare your heart.

It's time for a reality check. You've just made an outrageous ask of some of your closest friends. It's outrageous because it's exactly the kind of thing that most of us don't talk about. We want our friends to like us and know us, but most of us really don't want to hear our friends' unvarnished opinions of us. Even more, most of us don't really want to give our unvarnished opinions. It doesn't feel safe.

You may get some strange responses back. If your friends and family aren't used to this kind of thing, expect weird responses. They may suspect you're up to something strange. One person doing this process was horrified to discover their family members all started calling each other wondering if they were being set up. A commitment to growth and a desire for honesty is not the norm in our culture.

You will also find that some number of the people you ask for feedback will simply never respond. This was my experience. I carefully selected a group of people that I thought would have great wisdom for me. I was taken aback, even a little bit hurt, when more than half of them didn't even acknowledge my request.

Be gentle with them. You've asked them to do something hard. Some of them have never thought about their own lives in this way, let alone yours. You're asking them to do something that—depending on the tone of your relationship—might feel dangerous. If you've been defensive in the past, or if you have a hard time listening, your friends will intuitively feel insecure about giving you this kind of feedback.

It's a near guarantee that some people just won't be able to help in this way. Don't feel bad about it, and don't make them feel bad about it. Just move on. Others will respond, and then you'll have great feedback.

"Feedback is the breakfast of champions," at least according to the popular coaching phrase. The truth is feedback is often a bitter breakfast. Hearing how other people really experience you is a difficult thing, especially if you let go of explaining and defending yourself. Other people often don't see your strengths in the same way you do. And of course, most of the time, other people see our weaknesses more clearly than we do. So, prepare yourself.

▸ **Remind yourself that this feedback represents their experience.**

They may be wrong. They may misunderstand you. Or they may think you're the greatest. Whatever they say, remember they are telling their own story. They are not saying what's true of you. Just what they have truly experienced.

▸ **Guard against the temptation to respond.**

The desire to explain ourselves is powerful. It's one of the ways we manage our reputation and sense of value. But you promised that you would be non-defensive and listen. So just do that. Don't engage in conversation over these things.

There's one exception. If this feedback reveals a situation in which you really hurt someone and didn't know about it, then you need to pursue that conversation and make it right. Otherwise, just listen.

▸ **Make a plan for how you'll process this feedback.**

I scheduled an appointment with my counselor so that I'd have the place to talk about what I learned and how it felt. If the feedback brings up painful or complicated emotions for you, spend time processing those feelings in your journal or in a safe relationship.

Along the way, consider this. Everything about this experience is data for you to process, not just the words on the paper. Think about these things:

- Did you have resistance or discomfort making the request?
- Did you have anxiety waiting for the responses?
- How many of your people chose to respond?
- How did that feel for you? Why?
- Did people have a clear sense of you? Why or why not?
- Was there agreement between them?
- How did the feedback make you feel? Good, bad, misunderstood?

This isn't just a list of tasks for you to complete. It's an experiment digging into your emotions and experiences to understand more clearly who you are. Processing how all of this feels is far more important than rushing through a list of tasks so that you can get to the final result.

4. Tag the feedback.

You asked your "mirrors" to give feedback identifying the top few motivations or values they see guiding you. Chances are good that they have already done the work of getting the idea down to a single word or short phrase, but if they didn't, you can do it for them.

If you need to do this, make sure the word or phrase you select honors the original intention of the feedback. Avoid the temptation to editorialize by choosing a word with more positive connotations than the feedback originally said.

You are ready to move on when you've gathered honest feedback from 8-10 people who know you well, and have gotten that feedback tagged with key words or short phrases, just as you did with your memories.

Take a deep breath. You're over the hump. You've just done one of the most difficult steps in personal growth—listening to the honest feedback of people around you. It only gets easier from here.

seven

Gather and Refine

Things which matter most must never be at the
mercy of things which matter least.

—*Johann Wolfgang von Goethe*

Now you've got everything you need. You may not see them yet, but your *authentic core values* are all sitting there right in front of you. Let's start identifying them.

Assignment 4

Gather and refine yourself

You presently have two raw lists. The first is your list of emotionally important memories, tagged with key words or short phrases. At the least, there should be fifty to seventy-five items in that list. The second is the list of feedback you got from other people. If you had eight to twelve people respond, giving you three to five top values or motivations each, you should have another forty to sixty items. That means you could have anywhere from a hundred to two hundred statements about who you are or how you're experienced.

First we're going to gather the focusing words together into a single list.

1. Gather yourself.

On a fresh journal page, begin gathering the tags, key words, and short phrases. Write them clearly in a single vertical column. Your goal is a single list of words or, at most, two-word phrases.

These things can be positive or negative. It doesn't matter. At this point they just needs to be clear. Don't worry about duplicates or similar ideas at this point. That's likely and good. We'll handle it later. There should be one entry for every memory and one for every piece of outside feedback.

Your list isn't getting shorter yet, just more concise. When I did this process, I ended up with a list several pages long.

When you're done, you have a snapshot of how you experience yourself and how others see you. That alone is a pretty significant thing, worth reflecting on and journaling through.

2. Weed the list.

At this point you ought to have a pretty lengthy list, maybe as many as a hundred or two hundred items. This is interesting, but it's far too long to provide focus. Plus, the list likely has some duplicates as well as some weeds.

Duplicates are obvious. This is where you or others used the very same word, or a synonym, to describe the motivation in different entries on your list. Shortly, we'll gather those together.

Weeds are more complicated. These are words on the list that simply do not resonate with your heart. They represent values that honestly aren't core motivations for you. Perhaps they are motivations you felt at certain points, but they are outliers in your life experience, not your normal response. Perhaps they are values that your "mirrors" noted, but their interpretation of your heart in that situation is just plain wrong. Feel free to cross out any of the words or phrases that you think are weeds.

Now, be careful! This is an easy place to derail your process. Be honest with yourself as you do this. You're not just crossing out words you don't like, or getting rid of the negative words just because they are negative. You could easily turn the list "aspirational," cutting the real motivations and keeping the ones you wish were true of you. Don't do that. It will undermine all the work you've done so far.

Your goal is to remove words from the list that you honestly believe aren't core motivations for you.

In my case, several words didn't seem to fit me. I wrote in my journal about each of them. I prayed about them. I even asked my therapist and my wife for input before I was willing to take them off the list.

3. Name the *themes*.

In your list you will find words and phrases that are similar or related ideas. These represent *themes* in your life. Group these together and select a single word that represents this theme. Choose a word that resonates with you.

In my case, the following showed up on my list:

- "Forgiveness." (This showed up ten times in my memory list.)

- "Marc values grace." (This was reported by two of my outside feedback people.)

- "Giving second chances." (This was a single entry but similar in concept.)

- "Letting people off the hook." (This was a single entry, but also similar.)

- "Redemption." (This was on my list once.)

My therapist and I decided that the word "redemption" best represented this collection of words. It seemed to be an authentic motivation in my life. This *theme* covered a number of duplicates, as well as drew together some similar entries.

One important thing to pay attention to: If you had the same word or similar ideas in your list multiple times, it's a *theme* you've seen recur. If more than one of your outside feedback responses contains the same theme, this is something that others see very clearly in you. Make a note of which themes have this kind of support behind them. The more times a duplicate shows up on your list, the more present and powerful that theme is for you.

4. Prioritize your list.

Now you've weeded the list, gotten rid of duplicate entries, and identified the themes, you should have a list of motivations or values made up of your new themes, as well as any single entries that didn't make it into a theme category. The entire list is single words or very short phrases.

We're getting closer! There's one last step in shortening your raw list before we identify your *authentic core values*. You need to prioritize the list. For this you'll need one additional tool, a stack of Post-it notes or index cards.

Now follow these steps:

1. Write each value, motivation, or theme word on a single Post-it note or card. Each card will have a single word or phrase on it.

2. Lay the cards out on a table where you have lots of room to move them around.

3. Begin by picking up any two cards. Compare them and decide which concept moves you more powerfully. Which of the two motivations or values has shown up more in your life? Which one seems more central to your heart? Be honest. Don't pick the one you wish was more powerful in your life. Don't pick the one that seems more positive or honorable. (Don't worry! Even if seemingly negative values make it into the list. We'll talk about how that can be a positive part of your growth.)

4. Lay the two cards on the table, creating a scale, the more powerful motivation to your right. Your goal is to end up with all the cards in a single row, in order from least to most moving to your heart, from left to right.

5. Now pick up a single new card. Compare it to the cards you already laid down in your scale. Where would this new card fall? Is it more important than the most important one? Does it fall between them? Add it into the scale in the spot that seems most accurate to you.

6. Continue this process until all of the cards have been prioritized and added to your scale. Compare each card to the ones on either side. **If you were in a situation that pitted motivation A against motivation B, which one would prevail?** Again, you're not choosing which one you wish would win. You're choosing which one you believe would actually move you, based on your history.

7. After you've worked through all the cards, scan through them one last time and make sure the scale from left to right seems accurate to you. Make any final adjustments in the order of the cards until you feel that you've got the most accurate order you can have.

5. Write your short list.

Crack open your journal to a fresh page. Looking at your scale of cards, write the motivations or values in order from highest to lowest. Now draw a line after the fifth one. Everything above this line, from one to five, is your short list. If you've been honest and done your homework, your *authentic core values* are in this list.

We're almost done. The next step is to put some thought into molding these words into powerful tools for shaping your future life. Before we go there, what happens if you had some values make it onto your list that aren't all that positive?

eight

Look Past the Shadow to the Light

We are all like the bright moon, we still have our darker side.

—Khalil Gibran

In Chapter 2 we talked about the difference between aspirational values, imposed from the outside in, and authentic values, which emerge from the inside out.

The benefit of aspirational values is that we get to pick them. That means we probably would never pick something negative. ("Woohoo! I'm choosing a core value of Insecurity," said no one ever.) But aspirational values can often get in the way of your growth, because they aren't really who you are. If you're going to grow, you've got to start where you actually are.

Authentic core values will resonate with you because they are a part of you. They will more easily inspire you, because they already have been inspiring you.

But there's one problem. You may have come across something you didn't expect. You might find you have a core motivation that you don't really like, or that isn't helpful for the kind of life you want. What then?

Here's an example from my life. As I did this work, I found a disconcerting theme. I have an unfortunate and painful need to be liked. Throughout my life, I've always felt a bit on the outside. The result of this was a desire to be included. To be included, you have to be liked. This motivation has been a hurdle in my life in many ways. It has impacted my relationships. At times, it has led me to compromise my integrity.

This theme is a part of my life. I could see it clearly when I looked back at my *emotionally important moments*. It showed up in the feedback I got from others. It's something that has been a powerful motivation in my life.

Is it a core value? It has certainly driven me. But it's not who I want to be. It's not who I believe God made me to be. It's certainly not an ideal I aspire to!

What do I do?

The back side of light

A lot of reflection and conversation with my counselor led me to understand something that shifted my perspective, allowing me to see something positive in this dark place of insecurity. My painful longing to be liked is actually a *shadow*. By that I mean that it is the dark side of something light and good.

My story (my life experiences) and *my wiring* (my innate self, how God made me) have led me to have a deep need and value for community. My feelings of not belonging are a symptom of something bigger. My desire to be liked is an attempt to address this pain, but it's a flawed response. It grows out of insecurity, fear, and selfishness. The light on the other side of this *shadow* is a desire for community.

With this realization, I was able to see that this has been a part of my life all along. As a child I drew people around me. As a teenager, I found enormous purpose working at summer camp, creating community with the staff and for the kids. In a hundred different ways —with roommates, church groups, a community household, and in my work as a pastor—I have invested time and energy trying to create community. Sometimes it was healthy; sometimes not.

What does this mean? At the root of this painful part of my life lies an authentic core value. With restoration and healing, this can become life giving for me and for the people around me. The same is true for you.

So how can you find the value behind the shadow?

Optional Assignment
The light behind the shadow

Here's a journal exercise that can help you start making this shift.

1. Name the shadow.

Identify the motivation that has shown up as a theme in your life that doesn't seem positive. For me, the shadow in this case is "wanting to be liked." It could be any powerful theme that has shown up in your life over and over, bringing you pain.

Common shadows include comfort seeking, need for control, or a desire for affirmation. We all struggle with these, but that's not the point. Has one of these drives recurred powerfully in your life, taking you away from health and wholeness?

2. Identify the need.

Every *shadow* is a flawed or inauthentic way of trying to fulfill a need. We only do things repeatedly that pay off for us in some way. So what is it about this thing that "works" in your life?

Begin with a prayer of availability, asking God to give you insight into this area of brokenness in your life. Then brainstorm in your journal about what need this shadow motivation might fill for you.

In my case, the drive to be liked often governed my choices and relationships. I'd make commitments that I shouldn't have. Why? Because people respond positively when you give them a "Yes." I'd avoid conflict even when it was necessary because confrontation is uncomfortable for people. There were times when I'd shade the truth in my favor during conversations if it seemed to resonate positively with the people I was with.

Of course, all of these things had negative consequences in my life, so you could argue that they didn't "work." But in the moment, face-to-face, these choices satisfied that urgent need to be liked. If people liked me, they would want to be around me. That's what "worked" for me. The need behind the scenes was my need to belong.

Identifying the need behind the shadow can be difficult, especially if you've not spent much time in reflection on your own life. This is a spot in the process where it may be necessary to get some outside guidance. It could be as simple as having a conversation with a discerning friend. It could be something that you talk through with a professional counselor.

3. Reframe the value.

Every healthy need in us can be connected to a positive value. Think about the need you have. What positive value might lie behind it? Journal on the possibilities.

The need that surfaced for me was belonging. However, belonging isn't something you can do on your own in a vacuum. Belonging is a relational reality. To belong, you have to have someone or some group to belong to. My need to belong pointed toward a desire for safe, inclusive community.

4. Ask if it resonates.

Look back at your story and your emotionally important memories. Reflect on whether this reframed positive value has been a part of your life in the past. Does it resonate with you now?

Probably all of us have a desire or a need for belonging and community. For me this motivation showed up so frequently in my story that it seemed fair to call it a value. A desire to build and be a part of community has led me to make quite a number of decisions—both good and bad in my life.

Keep working until you come up with a positive value that resonates with you. If you can't, then go back to step 3 and dig deeper. When you find a positive value that resonates, you can use this new positive value to reframe the negative motivation. Once it's restated in this positive way, you have an authentic value that can help you in thinking about your future.

In my case, any future that is life giving will include the chance for me to be a community builder, where I get to help other people find belonging and acceptance. It's no longer about being liked. It's about giving a gift to others that has been so crucial to me.

Finding this is a kind of small miracle. This is redemption, when God takes your broken places and uses them to bring blessing to the people around you.

This is healing work

This reframing process is actually a step of healing. This is not just a word game. God is at work in this.

When we understand the flawed responses we choose and why they seem so natural to us, we can step out from under their control. We can't begin to choose differently until this happens. Best of all, when we can see the positive value or need deep within, we can embrace it.

I still act out of insecurity and a desire to be liked, but I beat up on myself much less. I try to remember that this is my need for community surfacing. That's a need built into me, something God given. It's a good thing. I can set aside the fear and insecurity and make sure I'm meeting that need without compromising good boundaries or violating who I am. You can do the same.

nine

Shape the Words That Shape You

*The difference between the almost right word
and the right word is really a large matter—'tis
the difference between the lightning bug
and the lightning.*

—Mark Twain

You've come a long way. You have in front of you five words or short phrases, but these are much more than vocabulary.

These words are a rich description distilled from the several hours of self-reflection you've invested and the feedback of people who know you well. They represent motivations that have surfaced in your life or been visible to others over and over again—many of them since you were a child. If some of these words were negative, you had to dig deep to discover the positive value behind the shadow. These words are rich, deep, powerful, and personal to you.

Now you get to take these words and identify the values that you want to guide your choices into a better future.

Assignment 5

Shaping the Words

Look at the five words or phrases in front of you. If you've done the process honestly, these are very close to your *authentic core values*. They may all be wonderful things that inspire you. They also may not be. Either way, they are truly the motivational themes that have been present in your life and shaped the choices you've made.

Without reflection, these motivations will continue to function in your life. That's what they do. They are a part of you and they move you. Now you have the opportunity to shape where those values can take you in the future.

1. Pick your "working core values."

Before we go on, look over your list. All five may be meaningful to you, but five isn't a magic number. Evaluate where you want to focus as you move into the future. If some are more important to you than others, you can narrow the list. Pick at least three of these areas. Whatever you pick, this will be your working list of core values.

2. Write each value statement.

For each of these values, write a short statement that expresses the heart of the value. It should only be a sentence or two. Your goal is to express what the value means to you in a way that can help you focus in the future. You can find this sentence more easily by asking yourself two questions:

- ▸ Why is this value important to me?
- ▸ What good thing does this value bring into my life?

In my work I found a theme of forgiveness and second chances. I gave this theme the label of Redemption. Redemption is important to me because it opens the possibility for new chances, new opportunities, and better relationships. The good thing this brings into my life is a better future with better relationships. I communicated those two ideas in this sentence:

> ### *Redemption.*
> *Forgiveness creates the opportunity for people, relationships, and opportunities to be restored, opening the door to a better future.*

Go ahead and do this for each of your values. Keep working on these sentences until they work for you. The final result needs to move you. These sentences should raise your pulse a bit as you think about how life could be. These are unique and precious to you, so put in the time to get them right.

3. Create your Authentic Core Value document.

Now you've got your 3—5 core values and a concise statement explaining each one. You've done amazing work. Compile these statements onto a page that you can put on your wall, in your planner, on your computer, and in your journal. In the next chapter we'll talk about more things you can do to help these values be active in your life.

Note to Christians

An unfortunate and all-too-common tendency among Christians is to think that their core values ought to be things like "the Bible," "Worship," and "Obeying God." These are fine things, but they are altogether useless as core values.

To say that you value the Bible says nothing about your actions. You can't do a value of "the Bible." You can have a value of learning the Bible. You could have a value of trying to live in alignment with the Bible. But even these statements are most often religious "oughts" and not *authentic core values.*

Instead of just saying that you value the Bible, it will be much closer to the truth to look at your actions to determine whether or not you value the Bible. I've met a good number of people who knew sizable parts of the Bible by memory and could speak intelligently on a wide number of biblical topics, but their life choices and attitudes demonstrated clearly that they didn't value the Bible in any way that altered how they lived.

For followers of Jesus, all our core values ought to come to represent Him in some way, but that's the life-long process of discipleship and spiritual growth, what the old theologians called sanctification. To list the top five things that Christians ought to be doing as your values doesn't serve you well. Core values are not "oughts." Core values are the authentic motivations that shape your decisions before you think about them too much.

It is my belief that if you are giving God access to your life in prayer, scripture, worship, and community, your character will be shaped. That means your core values will shift and come to reflect more of Jesus' character. This is part of the process of having your mind renewed that we see in Romans 12:2.

If you still feel a need to have your faith represented in your core value statement in some way, I suggest two things, both of which I did in my process. Write a Spiritual Focus Statement and pick a Motivating Scripture.

Optional Assignment
Write a Spiritual Focus Statement

This is an opportunity for you to connect the dots explicitly between your core values and your spiritual commitment. Instead of wedging spiritual ideas into your core values, you can do something more authentic. Think about who you want to be spiritually, and reflect on how your core values lead toward this.

You can get a sense of direction by asking the following questions of each of your values:

▸ Where and how do I see this value reflected in the life of Jesus?

▸ If I lived out of these values, how would that help me follow Jesus better?

After reflecting and perhaps journaling on these things, write a paragraph about the connection between your core values and your spiritual intentions.

I ended up with four core values: Belonging, Redemption, Creative Intentionality, and Growth. All of these connect deeply to my spiritual journey. This is how I expressed that connection:

Spiritual Focus

As a follower of Jesus, I find these values embodied in His life and message. His grace creates a safe and belonging place for me to live from, where I can be truthful about my own limitations and weaknesses. His missional call motivates me to share these values with others through my words, my actions, and the things I create. His example challenges me to live firmly from my own beliefs and truth, while always speaking and acting in love. I believe the church is meant to be a place where others can experience these same things through and because of Jesus.

Optional Assignment

Choose a Motivating Scripture

This process should have given you ample time to reflect on your life and who you are. Find a passage of Scripture that expresses a sense of what's most important to you. Look to your core values for a direction. This is more than a favorite verse or one that deeply encourages you. You are looking for a passage that connects with your heart and provides biblical motivation for who you want to be.

If you aren't familiar enough with the Bible to bring up a verse from memory, there are a lot of tools you can use to help you find the right verse. Here are two quick and easy-to-use options:

- **Search "Bible verses about _____" with your favorite Internet search engine.** Quite a number of Web sites have compiled lists of Scripture by topic. This won't get you a comprehensive list, but it will give you a good start.

- **Do a word search at www.BibleGateway.com.** You can enter different key words and find all the verses in the Bible that use that word. You can also limit the search to specific parts of the Bible, like the Gospels (for the words of Jesus), or the Epistles (for Paul's letters), or the New Testament. That's a big help if you remember loosely where the verse is that you want but not the specific book.

The verse that motivates me the most deeply and ties into my core values is Ephesians 2:10. *"For we are his workmanship, created in Christ Jesus for good works, which God prepared beforehand, that we should walk in them."*

This verse expresses my belief that we are each uniquely crafted by God, that we each have a God-given purpose, and that our life is most fulfilling when we are living out of that purpose. But that's my verse. You go find your own!

ten

Letting Your Core Values Work

Don't ask what the world needs. Ask what makes you come alive, and go do it. Because what the world needs is people who have come alive.

—Howard Thurman

Now you're looking at a crisp, newly printed page with your freshly crafted core values on it. You didn't just make these words up. They aren't empty hopes. They are words that accurately represent your heart. They move you. They have the potential to help shape an incredible future.

You may have spent hours reflecting and carefully crafting your core values statement. What happens once the words are chosen and sentences formed? Do the words get stuck in your journal or in some dark corner of the documents folder on your computer? Do they end up printed on a piece of fancy paper and hung on your wall?

If that's true, then your core values are not serving you well. You put a lot of time and heart into those words. Used properly, core values can be transformative in your life. So, how are you going to use your core values?

Core values do something important. They provide direction, like a compass. They help limit choices, like a water filter. They have the ability to call you home to your true God-given self, like a homing pigeon.

But a compass only helps when you look at it. A water filter only works when it's in the flow. Homing pigeons only find their way home when they listen to that deep instinct.

So, how do you get your core values to be "in the flow" of your life and decisions? You review them, incorporate them, and evolve them. Let's look at how.

Review your values

Choices present themselves in our thinking all the time. If you've done a good job drilling down to your *authentic core values*, they will guide your choices without you even thinking about it. Because this filtering is happening automatically, you don't have the chance to reflect and choose the best path. This is when the shadow side of our values can come out. We live by reaction rather than intentional response or action.

The best outcome is available to you when you are conscious of your core values while you are reflecting on your course of action. If you review your core values regularly, you will be more conscious of them.

Here are several ways to do this:

▸ **Read your Core Values Daily.** This is most helpful when your core values are new to you or when you find yourself in a chaotic or complicated season where you're desperate for focus. Read through your core values every morning. This helps you learn them. It also serves as an affirmation of the kind of day you want to have. It's like checking your compass before you start walking.

You can find four examples that I created for my own core values here: www.marcalanschelske.com/core-value-word-art/

▶ **Build value muscle.** Pick one value for a season—a month, a quarter—and invest in that area. Read a book that aligns with that value. Do a topic study in the Bible, finding passages and stories that connect with your value. Try one activity that's out of the normal routine for you that emerges from that value. Choose a simple, repeatable act that demonstrates that value and commit to doing it five times a day for a week. As you do these and similar things, journal about what you are learning.

The more you intentionally practice actions in your life that you connect to your values in your mind, the easier and more natural this process becomes. You form habits simply by doing the same things over and over. Once something becomes habitual, it's been wired into your brain, and will only continue to be easier for you to do.

Evolve your values

You are not static and unchanging. You are constantly having new experiences that shape your worldview. Because your core values are a part of you, that means they shift as well.

Sometimes they shift through entropy and apathy. This kind of shift takes you away from who you want to be. Other times you learn powerful lessons and your values strengthen. Your essential core values will probably stay similar, but these life experiences will shift and focus them. It's important that your statement of core values keeps up with who you are becoming.

Set aside a block of time once a year for an annual re-visioning of your core values. Think through each value. How has this value guided you this past year? Where has it led you? Does it still resonate with you? Is the word choice still the best for everything you've learned? As you grow, your picture of the future may shift as well.

Don't let your core values die on a sheet of paper somewhere. Get the sentences you crafted into your head. Get them on your wall.

Find pictures, sculptures, or other memorabilia that bring them to mind. Get intentional about growing and practicing your values.

As you choose practices like these or others that make the most sense to you, over time your core values will become a natural awareness as you relate to the decisions and priorities in your life.

eleven

A Final Word

*Twenty years from now you will be more
disappointed by the things that you didn't do
than by the ones you did. So throw off the
bowlines. Sail away from the safe harbor.
Catch the trade winds in your sails.
Explore. Dream. Discover.*

—Mark Twain

How will you choose?

You are already living by some set of core values, and in reaction to the values and agendas of the people around you. But that's not what you were made for.

Living an intentional life comes from building mental and practical habits. Habits come from repeated behavior. You will repeat behavior that is important to you. This is the path to a well-lived life. Aristotle famously said, "We are what we repeatedly do. Excellence, then, is not an act but a habit." An excellent life comes because you choose it.

Core values are a tool to help you make these kinds of excellent, life-giving choices.

When I'm presented with options, if I am aware of my personal core value of Growth, I will always consider the choice that offers the most chance of personal development. My value is acting like a compass pointing me in the right direction. It may not be the way I want to go in the moment, but my value is there reminding me of the path I want to travel.

Sometimes our values rule out certain options. My value of Redemption means that holding a grudge is just not on the menu for me. My value is acting like a filter, screening out choices that aren't in alignment with my best self. I'm motivated to resolve conflicts early, to pursue healthy relationships, and to let go of insults. If I find myself holding something against someone, I know that I'm out of alignment with who I want to be, and I have immediate work to do.

If I go too long without doing real creative work, my energy level sinks and I find myself wrestling with motivation. Because I've identified Creative Intention as a core value, I am reminded to keep this part of myself active. Like a homing pigeon, this value draws me back to my best self.

In every case I can choose differently because of my awareness. I can choose to fill my life with commitments and obligations so I have no time to create. I can choose to let relationships stay broken. I can take the easy path of what I know, avoiding growth, because it's uncomfortable. But these are choices that move me away from who I want to be, even who I believe God is calling me to be. When I move away from that, I jeopardize the better future I want for me and for my family.

Your values are different from mine, but this process is the same for you.

Now, you've done the hard work of identifying your authentic inside-out core values. These words resonate with who you are and can help shape a great future. That's something to celebrate.

But the work is not over. In fact, it's just beginning.

Will you make the choice to live these values out? Will you choose practices that help your values find a concrete expression in your life and space? Will you hold your choices up against your values and evaluate your sense of direction?

If you will do these things, then a value-led life awaits you. Every day is an opportunity to become more the kind of person you hope to be.

The more you live in alignment with who God made you to be, the more fulfilling your life will be, regardless of the circumstances you find yourself in. You will be living according to your own *authentic core values*, undeterred by the competing agendas of the people around you.

You have the chance to make a difference in the world in a way that is perfectly suited for who you are—the good and beautiful purpose God planted in you from the beginning.

Glossary of Terms

Aspirational Core Values - Core Values that an individual or organization aspire to. Essentially they wish these values were true of them. Also called "Outside-In" core values because they are imposed externally, rather than reflecting an internal reality. In the best case, aspirational values can serve as an inspiration. In the worst case, they are a form of denial getting in the way of identifying the true motivations at work.

Authentic Core Values - Core Values that emerge from who the individual or organization truthfully is. Our behavior is already driven by these central motivations. Also called "Inside-Out" core values because they are an outward and visible expression of an inward truth.

Core Values - The central, most important motivations that drive an individual or organization.

Emotionally Important Moment - This phrase is used in this guide to identify any important choice or turning point in your life you can remember clearly. These moments are memorable because they contained some emotionally important content that has shaped you in some way.

Evernote - The best online note and journal tool available. It's cloud-hosted which means you can access it from any computer or device. You can store any kind of note or PDF as well as images and video. All your notes are fully indexed for searching and can be organized by notebook and tags. The basic account is free. This will more than serve most people's needs. Evernote is the cornerstone of my paperless office, and I can't recommend it more highly. Check it out at http://evernote.com

Inside-Out Core Values - See Authentic Core Values.

Journal - As used in this guide, a journal is some kind of tangible document where you write to process and understand your life. It can be a blank book, a lined notebook, a word processing document on your computer, or any number of other things. It's not a diary in the sense that you capture the details and events of your life. It doesn't require special writing skills or need to be carefully crafted. It is a private place where you write your thoughts, reactions and emotions. This very act helps you to formulate and understand them better. Even if you never read the contents of your journal again, simply writing will help you think more clearly, and more clearly understand the things you feel.

Moleskine Journal - Moleskine is a particular brand of blank book journals, with a long history of being favored by authors and artists. The books are very high quality with archival paper. They are one of the best options you can find. Moleskines are sold at bookstores and online at http://www.moleskine.com/us/

Outside-In Core Values - See Aspirational Core Values.

Shadow - Carl Jung pioneered the use of this word in the arena of psychology and personality. For him the shadow referred to those parts of us that we feel are unacceptable. Often this belief is created through trauma, disappointment, abuse and strict socialization. These unacceptable parts of ourselves we deny, shun, repress or ignore, often while overreacting to the very same tendencies in others.   In this guide, however, the word is used much more simply, without requiring anyone to subscribe to all of Jung's paradigm. Here shadow is a metaphor to help clarify that there are parts of us that we are ashamed of, but that every shadow is a flawed or inauthentic way of trying to fulfill what is often very real and good need that we have.

Theme - In this guide a theme is a set of similar motivations that you see recurring in your life. The more frequently the theme shows up in your homework, the more present and powerful it is for you.

Your Story - As used in this guide, this phrase has a particular meaning. Your story is the narrative of your life including the significant events that happened to you as well as the meaning you took from those events. It includes the who, what, where and when of your life, but more than that, it includes your emotional experience and the deep internal drivers that have shaped you. When you understand your story, you have some insight into why you behave the way you do. When your story goes unexamined, it is very often the case that you end up living out old patterns from your story without even understanding it. A good therapist is able to help you see and understand your story.

Your Wiring - This phrase refers to all the parts of your personality that are intrinsic to who you are by way of temperament, DNA, basic brain chemistry, biology, and all the other elements of personality that are more or less fixed at birth. This is the "hand you were dealt," as it were. In contrast, your story refers to the parts of your personality that emerge from the events of your life and the meaning you made of those events. Your wiring just is what it is; your story on the other hand is constructed.

Thanks for reading!

The process I've just shared with you was invaluable for me, and I hope you've found it helpful as well. If so, I'd love to hear your stories. I'm serious.

- Stop by my blog at www.MarcAlanSchelske.com, where I write about discovering and living out the good and beautiful life God has for you. Be sure to leave a comment, and sign up for my email updates.

- Email me at marc@MarcAlanSchelske.com. If you take the time to email, I'll take the time to respond.

- Follow me on Twitter www.twitter.com/schelske

- Or Facebook www.facebook.com/schelske

- Or even Google+ http://gplus.to/schelske

- Or even on Pinterest, where I'm busy posting pictures of my favorite wedding dresses . . . I kid, I kid. http://pinterest.com/marcschelske

Courage to you on your adventure!

Made in the USA
Monee, IL
26 October 2022

16592315R00042